P9-EGM-673

The BOY Who LOOKeD Like LiNCOLN

For Ken, Ted, Max, Tom, Bob, Sam & Al.—M.R.

For Brian; a Lincoln kinda guy—honestly.—D.C.

Text
copyright © 2003 by Mike Reiss.
Illustrations copyright © 2003 by David
Catrow. All rights reserved.

Designed by Debbie Guy-Christiansen
and Giovanni Cipolla.

Published by Price Stern Sloan,
a division of Penguin Young Readers
Group, 345 Hudson Street, New
York, NY 10014.

Published simultaneously in Canada.
Printed in the USA.

Library of Congress
Cataloging-in-Publication Data
Reiss, Mike.
   The boy who looked like Lincoln /
by Mike Reiss ; illustrated by
David Catrow.
      p. cm.
Summary: Eight-year-old Benjy,
who resembles Abraham Lincoln, is
tired of being teased and always
being Lincoln in the school play,
but a special camp helps him to
appreciate his appearance.
[1. Self-esteem—Fiction. 2. Identity—
Fiction. 3. Schools—Fiction. 4. Camps—
Fiction.] I. Catrow, David, ill. II. Title.
PZ7.R2784 Bo 2003
[E]—dc21

2003004712

ISBN 0-8431-0271-3   A   B   C   D   E   F   G   H   I   J

The BOY Who LOOKED Like LINCOLN

By Mike Reiss
Illustrated by David Catrow

PSS!
PRICE STERN SLOAN

New York

My name is Benjy. I'm eight years old. I look a lot like Abe Lincoln.

People first noticed it
when I was a baby.

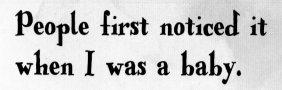

I guess I get it from my parents.

Every birthday
I get the same gifts.

I even wear the dumb hat. Anything else looks silly on me.

"Four score and SEVEN teeth ago..."

In every school play, I have to be Lincoln.
Even if he's not in the show.

But the worst part is the teasing.

So when school ended, I planned to spend the summer sitting in my room—in the dark.

But my parents had a surprise for me . . .

CAMP WHAT-CHA-MA-CALL-IT
The CAMP for KIDS who look like THINGS

They took me to a camp.
A special camp . . .

HONABE

MILLARD
FILLMORE
DAM

. . . A camp for kids who looked like things.

There was a kid who looked
like the Mona Lisa. And a kid
who looked like a frog. And one
who looked like a toaster.

There was even a kid who looked like the back of a horse. I felt really bad for him. But after a while, you didn't even notice.

We had fun
every day.

And at night, I'd stay up
late and read about Lincoln.
He was a pretty
cool guy.

I made a lot of friends that summer.

And so did the kid who looked like a horse's butt.

On the last day of camp my parents picked me up. "You look happy," said my Dad. "You need a haircut," said my Mom.

When I went back to school, I felt a lot better.

"I'm thinking how lucky I am to look like **Abe Lincoln**, our greatest president, who freed the slaves and won the Civil War and kept our country together and the capital of Nebraska is named after *him!*"

I guess your face is one thing
that makes you special.
I hope you like yours.
I know I like mine. . .

And I think it may have helped get me elected class president this year.

DETE

A Nit on every head

A Vote or Davies is A VOTE FOR SCABIES

The other CANDIDATE has Cooties

English Schminglish

PHOOEY

Tippecanoe ☆ AND ☆ pizza too!

Now I just have to figure out how to help my baby brother, Dickie.